Murat's Army

The Army of the Kingdom of Naples 1806-1815

Digby Smith

Plates by Henri Boisselier

Helion & Company Limited

Helion & Company Limited
26 Willow Road
Solihull
West Midlands
B91 1UE
England
Tel. 0121 705 3393
Fax 0121 711 4075
Email: info@helion.co.uk
Website: www.helion.co.uk
Twitter: @helionbooks
Visit our blog at http://blog.helion.co.uk/

Published by Helion & Company 2018
Designed and typeset by Farr out Publications, Wokingham, Berkshire
Cover designed by Paul Hewitt, Battlefield Design (www.battlefield-design.co.uk)
Printed by Henry Ling Limited, Dorchester, Dorset

Text © Digby Smith 2018
Images © Anne S.K. Brown Collection unless otherwise credited

Cover: Title page from *L'Armée Napolitaine 1806-1814* by Henri Boisselier, © Anne S.K. Brown Collection
Every reasonable effort has been made to trace copyright holders and to obtain their permission for the use of copyright material. The author and publisher apologise for any errors or omissions in this work, and would be grateful if notified of any corrections that should be incorporated in future reprints or editions of this book.

ISBN 978-1-912390-09-0

British Library Cataloguing-in-Publication Data.
A catalogue record for this book is available from the British Library.

All rights reserved. No part of this publication may be reproduced, stored in a retrieval system, or transmitted, in any form, or by any means, electronic, mechanical, photocopying, recording or otherwise, without the express written consent of Helion & Company Limited.

For details of other military history titles published by Helion & Company Limited, contact the above address, or visit our website: http://www.helion.co.uk

We always welcome receiving book proposals from prospective authors.

Contents

Introduction		4
The Plates		
1	The Kingdom of Naples and its Armed Forces	6
2	Staff Officers and Aides-de-Camp	12
3	The Royal Guard	20
4	The Line Cavalry	45
5	The Line Infantry	54
6	The Light Infantry	71
7	Technical Troops	81
8	Internal Security Forces	84
9	The Navy	114

Introduction

The study of the uniforms of the Kingdom of Naples under King Joachim Murat from 1808 to 1815 has long been recognized by those attempting it, as being a topic more problematic than that of almost any other state or period. This is largely due to the fragmentary state of the surviving documentation, its often contradictory nature, the frequency of the changes dictated by Murat during his brief reign, and the fact that some of these changes seem to have been only partially implemented, if at all.

French and German researchers have in the past recorded their frustrations as they grappled with these inconsistencies and the artist Henri Boisselier, whose paintings form the body of this work, compounded the puzzle on many occasions with his rather careless approach to the details of his subjects. Studying and interpreting Boisselier's paintings, I have been impressed by his energy, artistry and the volume of his work, but repeatedly frustrated and disappointed by his lack of discipline and ability to record important details. It is however noteworthy – and unusual – to see how many para-military and non-military organizations Boisselier included in his collection.

Henri Boisselier, was born in Paris on 13 April 1881. The son of a veteran of the Franco-Prussian War of 1870-1871, he studied at the Boulle school of fine art in Paris and became an art critic. His hobby was militaria, as was the case with the collector, Léonce Bernardin, the uniformologists Eugène Louis Bucquoy and Louis Fallou. Bosselier produced numerous watercolours in which the soldier-subject always has just the right feel and character of their time, as well as many of the uniform details. Bucquoy entrusted him with the production of many such plates intended to illustrate his works.

Boisselier also made contact with Herbert Knötel, son of the well-known German uniformologist Richard Knötel, for whom he drew some of the plates for the 'Neue Folge' (new series) of the *Uniformenkunde*, which Herbert Knötel published in order to complete his father's great work. In the late 1940s and 1950s, Boisselier produced many sets of uniform plates for various collectors. He also worked with the Society of Historical Figurine Collectors and was still actively participating in a meeting of SCFH on 12 September 1959, but three days later, while working on plates for the Society, he died suddenly.

Boisselier worked with pen, gouache and water colour and was known for the speed of his work, being able to draw a character in 15 to 20 minutes. Almost all his known plates contain detailed indications of the sources used. These included contemporary artists, such as the Martinet plates, works by Horace Vernet and Alfred-Charles-Adolphe de Marbot, diaries, and documents in various archives. While the French and foreign armies of the Napoleonic Wars were the main themes of his work, there are also series devoted to the armies of the Ancien Régime, the Restoration and the Second Empire – which benefited from the efforts of the artist's assistant, the Alsatian, Nussbaum. This collection of plates of the Neapolitan army is based on paintings held in the Museum of San Martino, a museum housed in a monastery in Naples, or upon uniform regulations.

As we will discover when examining these paintings of the army of the kingdom of Naples, Boisselier often glossed over the details. The emblems on shako plates, which are rightly regarded as being of considerable importance and justifying careful execution by an artist, are dashed off as squiggles, or the wrong royal cipher has been carelessly scribbled in, often without the obligatory royal crown surmounting it. There seem to have been three royal ciphers in use during King Joachim Murat's reign: 'J', 'JN' and 'GN'. The latter dating from 1813, when he apparently also used the Italian version of his name 'GIOACCHINO' and added 'NAPOLEONE' on coinage struck in the kingdom in that year. At least two cavalry standards, using this latter style, seem to have survived.

Boisselier is similarly over-tolerant in his use of 'grande tenue' and 'petite tenue' on the uniforms in his plates. Normally, grande tenue would be just the everyday petite tenue with the addition of cords and plumes to the shakos and bearskins.

INTRODUCTION

After Boisselier's death, his collections were dispersed; some of his works may still be found in flea markets, collectors' exchanges or on the EBay on-line sales site. Some of his works, including the series reproduced here, are preserved at the extremely impressive Anne S.K. Brown Military Collection. The plate numbers used in this book are the references used in that collection.

Digby Smith,
Thetford 2018

1

The Kingdom of Naples and its Armed Forces

The Kingdom of Naples was a state covering parts of the southern portion of the Italian peninsula from the Middle Ages to 1860. It was sometimes united politically with the island of Sicily. In 1442, Naples fell to the ruler of Sicily, King Alfonso V of Aragon, who in 1443 assumed the title 'King of the Two Sicilies' i.e., of Sicily and of Naples. He passed this title on to his son and grandson, Ferdinand I and Ferdinand II. There continued to be no overall political unification of the Italian peninsula; Naples was claimed by the French King Charles VIII, who held it briefly in 1495. In 1504 the Spanish won control of Naples and Sicily, which were ruled by viceroys for two hundred years. Under Spain the country was regarded merely as a source of revenue and experienced a steadily increasing taxation and economic decline. Provoked by this combination, the lower and middle classes finally rebelled in July 1647, in the Revolt of Masaniello, but the Spanish and the local barons combined to suppress the uprising in 1648.

As a result of the War of Spanish Succession (1701–14), the Kingdom of Naples passed under the influence of the Austrian Habsburgs. In 1715, Sicily was briefly held by the duchy of Piedmont and in 1734 the Spanish prince Don Carlos de Borbón (later King Charles III) conquered Naples and Sicily, which were then combined as a separate kingdom under the Spanish Bourbons. During the 18th century the Bourbon kings, in the spirit of enlightened despotism, sponsored reforms to rectify social and political injustices and to modernize the state.

The Bourbon King Ferdinand IV of Naples and Sicily, began a series of reforms late in the century, which coincided with the French Revolution of 1789, which had generated a flood of republican and democratic ideas across Europe. These ideas appealed strongly to those Neapolitan liberals – middle-class intellectuals, some of the nobility and the clergy – who suspected that the domestic Bourbon reforms were designed more to increase the king's power than to benefit the nation. 'Patriots' began to conspire against their government and were met with persecution. King Ferdinand's army joined the allied forces against republican France in the War of the Second Coalition (1798-1802) with disastrous results. Naples was seized by the French, and Ferdinand fled to the island of Sicily.

As the French approached Naples, frantic efforts were made to deny them anything of military value. If it could not be evacuated in time, efforts were made to destroy it. This included many of the vessels of the Neapolitan navy, the contents of the arsenal and the navy yard. Two ships-of-the-line, two frigates and dozens of smaller vessels were burned or scuttled in January of 1799. 24 January 1799, the Parthenopean Republic was proclaimed by the French to replace the feudal Kingdom of the Two Sicilies, but then their army withdrew and the infant republic was left unprotected. The city of Naples fell to Cardinal Fabrizio Ruffo's royalist forces in their counter-offensive on 13 June 1799, after desperate resistance by the republican patriots. This saw the end of the Parthenopean Republic. King Ferdinand returned to Naples.

As part of the terms agreed for the surrender of the city, the rebels had been promised their freedom to remain or to go into exile, but, on 24 June, Admiral Horatio Nelson's fleet arrived in the bay of Naples and Nelson was soon dabbling in the very murky waters of the local politics. In agreement with the royal powers on the island of Sicily, he repudiated the terms of the capitulation. Many captured republicans were then put to death, including Neapolitan Admiral Francesco Caracciolo. Ferdinand returned to mainland Naples, but his further machinations with the Austrians and British exasperated Napoleon.

Wanting to keep things quiet in southern Italy, Napoleon and Ferdinand had signed a treaty by which the French would evacuate Apulia, the heel of Italy. In return, the Kingdom of Naples would stay neutral in the impending War of the Third Coalition (1803-1806). No sooner had the French occupying forces left, than Ferdinand admitted British and Russian armies into his kingdom. On 2 December 1805, Napoleon's armies crushed the armies of Austria and Russia at the Battle of the Three Emperors at Austerlitz. This caused General Maurice Lacy and his 14,000 Russian troops to be recalled from Naples in January 1806 and to return to the island of Corfu, in the Adriatic. The British contingent also withdrew, leaving Ferdinand's kingdom exposed to French retribution.

THE KINGDOM OF NAPLES AND ITS ARMED FORCES

Napoleon moved quickly to fill the power vacuum in the region and in January 1806, a French army, led by Marshal André Masséna, set off from northern Italy for the Kingdom of Naples. The Neapolitan army, which went out to block this advance, was heavily defeated at the Battle of Campotenese on 10 March and rapidly disintegrated. The invasion was successful despite some setbacks: the capture of the island of Capri, just to the south of the Bay of Naples, by Sir Sidney Smith's marines and sailors in May 1806; the prolonged French siege of the Neapolitan fortress of Gaeta (28 February-18 July); the British victory at the Battle of Maida on 4 July; and a stubborn guerrilla war, waged by the peasantry against the French. Total success eluded the French because Ferdinand withdrew to the island of Sicily, where he was protected from them by the Royal Navy and a British Army garrison. On 30 March 1806, Napoleon appointed his brother, Joseph Bonaparte, to be the new King of Naples. When Joseph was given the crown of Spain, on 6 June 1808, Napoleon passed Naples on to his own brother-in-law Joachim Murat, who entered his new realm on 6 September 1808. Under the rule of the French, Neapolitan society had been modernized by the abolition of feudalism and the introduction of a uniform legal code, a revised taxation system, conscription, and other French revolutionary laws. Murat and his wife, Napoleon's sister Caroline, proved to be genuinely popular as king and queen.

Although Murat was on good terms with his new Neapolitan subjects, his relationship with Napoleon was soon placed under pressure. His predecessor, Joseph, had maintained a good relationship with the Emperor while in Naples because he presided over a normal Napoleonic satellite kingdom, which employed many French officials, operating according to French laws and regulations, all managed and exploited for the benefit of France. This had caused the relationship between Joseph and his subjects to be difficult at best.

Napoleon had expected that Murat would continue in a similar fashion. However, the new king and queen decided to adopt a more independent style. Although he maintained Napoleon's legal reforms, Murat attempted to limit the influence of the French officials, who had been imported into the government of Naples. He even went so far as to demand that the Frenchmen in his service take Neapolitan citizenship or face removal from office. Not surprisingly, Napoleon quickly vetoed this measure, but despite this reverse, native Neapolitan officials became quite powerful under Murat after having been restricted to holding only minor posts under Joseph.

The territory itself was politically restructured and was divided into fourteen provinces which were in turn subdivided into districts. The provincial and district councils included members appointed by the King. However, the local intellectual class did not support these reforms as enthusiastically as had been the case in the northern Italy. This lack of local input, coupled with financial stringency, limited the scope of the reforms achieved in Naples.

Recruitment of the new army was difficult from the start, due to the usual resistance to the unpopular French conscription system which had been introduced. The numbers of conscripts raised was initially so meagre, that regular recourse had to be had to drafting convicted criminals into the regiments. Most of the officers were captured enemy officers or French officers, transferred into Neapolitan service. The army ultimately consisted of the Royal Guard, fielding a division apiece of infantry and cavalry; twelve regiments of line infantry, each of three battalions; four regiments of light infantry; two regiments of chasseurs-à-cheval, later converted to Chevaulegers along with two new-raised regiments of the latter for a total of four; six squadrons of Gendarmes; a regiment of foot artillery; a battalion each of train, artificers, and armourers; and a battalion of sappers and miners. There were also fourteen Provincial Legions for internal security duties.

In October, 1808, the newly-appointed King Joachim Murat sent a force across the Bay of Naples and induced Sir Hudson Lowe to evacuate the island of Capri, together with his garrison of a battalion of Corsican Rangers and the Royal Maltese battalion, after less than a fortnight's siege. The British troops were released after swearing not to serve against France for a year. Murat thought to invade and capture Sicily in 1809, but his plans seem to have died on the drawing board. This cancellation was probably dictated by the flurry of crises which beset Napoleon's empire in that year, when the Emperor's attention was riveted on putting down Austria, Spain, Portugal, the British raid into the island of Walcheren, and some minor rebellions in northern Germany.

In February 1808 Napoleon's carefully-orchestrated plan to achieve control over Spain and Portugal rolled into motion. After much cunning manipulation of the utterly gullible Spanish royal family, they had agreed to allow tens of thousands of French troops into their kingdom, ostensibly as part of a plot, which they believed that they had hatched with Napoleon to invade Portugal and divide it into new Spanish and French provinces. But these French troops were commanded by generals with secret instructions to seize control of the key Spanish border fortresses, to ease the main French invasion force, which would quickly subdue the entire kingdom.

Italian and Neapolitan troops made up part of Général de Division Duhesme's VII Corps in Catalonia, in Général de Division Guiseppe Lechi's 2nd Division. On 29 February 1808, Lechi's division seized the fortress of Barcelona from the unsuspecting Spaniards. Similar coups secured other vital fortresses for the French and all seemed to be done and dusted. Then, on 2 May, the Spanish populace of Madrid rose up and attacked the French troops in the city, starting that vicious war of attrition, assassination and reprisal that was to drain so much of the French military's efforts – and their treasury – until 1814.

There were two features of the campaign in Spain, which affected all French troops – and their allies – in the kingdom. Firstly, there was the shortage of food and drink. This was caused by a complete inability of the French army to organize and maintain an effective ration re-supply system. Officers and men alike were all expected to live off what they could find, wherever they happened to be. The other factor was the total lack of any safe space for any member of their forces, despite the string of crushing victories that French generals achieved against the Spanish army. The ubiquitous guerrillas would ambush and murder even company-sized units on a regular basis. If a garrison was left to hold a post along the lines of communication, it could only survive by immediately constructing a robust defensive position and maintaining a stock of food and water within it. If they dropped their guard, even for a moment, they would be overrun and massacred.

The Neapolitan troops were employed almost constantly on similar operations aimed at stamping out guerrilla activity in the wild terrain of the province. They took part in Général de Brigade Schwarz's punitive expedition to Manresa, some 40 km from Barcelona, up in the hills; on their way there, they were ambushed and sent running back to the city. At this, the whole province exploded into open rebellion and a second expedition to Manresa suffered the same fate as the first, and lost over 400 casualties as well. Duhesme's next project was to take the city of Girona, which controlled his communications along the main road back up into France. The city was about 50km from Barcelona. He set off with Lechi's division, but with no siege artillery. After arriving before Girona on 20 June, he tried two quick assaults, both of which were easily beaten off with loss. Duhesme went back to Barcelona.

On 4 July 1808, Chabran's Italians and Neapolitans were again sent off into the hills, to clear out the guerrillas. At Granollers, 30km north of Barcelona, Chabran was confronted by guerrilla leader Francisco Milans, soundly trounced and sent running back for Barcelona yet again. Duhesme's troops were now cut off from France by land; he sent off a cry for help by a small boat, hugging the coast to avoid being taken by the ubiquitous Royal Navy, and Napoleon grudgingly sent more troops, under Général de Division Count Honoré-Charles Reille, to Catalonia.

Duhesme, who now had six siege guns, planned to meet up with Reille's division before Girona and to take that city. The two Franco-Italian-Neapolitan divisions reached Girona on 23 July 1808 and the second siege of the place began. Unluckily for the French, Dupont's French corps had capitulated to the Spanish under General Francisco Castaños at Bailen on 22 July and when the news reached Girona, it affected the morale of the combatants on both sides dramatically, but in opposite directions.

Now that most of the garrison of Barcelona was around Girona, the Spanish launched an attack on the reduced garrison, under Lechi, which he had trouble beating off. There was also a garrison of 150 Neapolitans in the small coastal fortress of Mongat, 10km north of the city, on the main coast road. On 31 July 1808 it was attacked by the Spanish miqueletes and by HMS *Impérieuse* (38) under Lord Cochrane. The fort was taken and destroyed, the garrison was taken prisoner, and Cochrane then destroyed the coast road with explosives. All communications between Barcelona and France would now have to pass along the rough, minor roads of the interior, running the inevitable gauntlet of the guerrillas.

On 16 August 1808, Duhesme had again had enough; he abandoned the second siege of Girona and returned to Barcelona. On 17 August he was sacked by Napoleon and replaced by Général de Division Count Laurent Gouvion St-Cyr, who was also reinforced by the divisions of Pino and Souham. Instead of the original 10,000 troops, with which Napoleon had thought that he could subdue and hold Catalonia, there were now 40,000 men there and they controlled merely the ground upon which they stood.

Girona was to be besieged for a third time, from 6 May to 12 December 1809, when it finally fell to the French who were now under Marshal Augereau. This badly botched operation involved most of VII Corps, a total of over 34,000 men, of whom over 15,000 died, mainly due to starvation and disease. The Spanish garrison of 9,371 men, under the inspirational General Don Mariano Alvarez, lost 5,122 men.

In March 1810 the Neapolitans were employed at the blockade of the Spanish-held fortress of Hostalrich, in the hills, midway between Barcelona and Girona, which was abandoned by its garrison on 12 May. Augereau was replaced in command of VII Corps by Marshal Macdonald on 22 May 1810. In the September of that year, the Spanish mounted a series of well-coordinated raids on isolated garrisons of VII Corps. The Neapolitans were employed on endless counter-insurgency operations and at the siege of Tortosa from 16 December 1810 to its fall on 2 January 1811. The Neapolitans were now transferred to the siege of Sagunto, which fell on 26 October 1811.

In 1811 the 1st and 2nd Neapolitan Line Infantry Regiments and the 1st Light Infantry were in Compère's division of Suchet's army in Valencia and the 2nd Neapolitan Chasseurs-à-Cheval were in his cavalry. On 15 December 1811 the 1st and 2nd Neapolitan Line and the 1st Light Infantry Regiments, being so reduced in strength, were combined into the 'new' 8th Neapolitan Line Infantry Regiment and cadres of officers were sent back to Naples to recruit new battalions for the three old regiments. The 8th Line was given the title 'Principe Luciano'. In 1812 and 1813 the Neapolitan troops were still in Suchet's army, in Musnier's 1st Division, together with the 1st Chasseurs-à-Cheval. In August 1813, at the time of Murat's defection to the allies, the Neapolitan troops still in Spain were disarmed and interned. After repatriation to Naples in 1814, these men became the new 11th Line Infantry Regiment.

For the invasion of Russia in 1812, Naples provided Général de Division Francois Destrees' 33rd Division of Marshal Pierre Augereau's XI Corps, consisting of the Marines of the Neapolitan Guard, the Velites à Cheval and à Pied, the Gardes d'Honneur, the 5th, 6th and 7th Line Infantry Regiments and two batteries of artillery. They formed part of the garrison of the port-city of Danzig (now Gdansk) on the Baltic Sea coast. Following the retreat of the remnants of the Grande Armée from Russia in late 1812, Murat, who had been left in command of what was left when Napoleon abandoned it on 5 December 1812, also threw in the towel, handed command on again to Eugene de Beauharnais, Viceroy of Italy, and returned to his kingdom.

Joachim Murat returned to Napoleon's side in Germany in August 1813, after calculating that the Emperor's old star was yet in the ascendant. In 1813 the Neapolitan regiments serving in Germnay remained in garrison in Danzig, but their elite companies took to the field as the Neapolitan Elite Regiment, brigaded with the 4th Light Infantry as part of the 31st Division, XI Corps. The Elite Regiment fought at Lutzen and the whole brigade took part in the defence of Leipzig.

King Joachim Murat abandoned Napoleon's cause again after the battle of Leipzig and returned to Naples. He formally defected to the allies on 11 January 1814 in return for being allowed to retain his throne and of providing 30,000 troops to support the allies against the French in Italy. He dragged his feet disgracefully in prosecuting offensive action against the French, before being finally goaded by his new Austrian allies into attacking the Franco-Italians at the River Taro, 10km west of Parma, in northern Italy, with an Austro-Neapolitan force on 13 April 1814. He was victorious in this minor clash and the Franco-Italians withdrew to Piacenza, where a small rearguard action took place next day. This marked the end of the fighting in Italy, as news of Napoleon's abdication now arrived. Murat was able to reach an agreement with Austria and the other allies, by which he retained the throne of Naples.

In 1815, news of Napoleon's arrival in France reached Naples on 4 March. Murat was already in secret negotiations with the court in Vienna to secure his hold on his throne and even Britain had signalled that they would not object to his continued presence. Napoleon somehow learned of what was going on. Ten days later, Murat had decided to support his old emperor and had declared war on Austria. At the head of 46,829 infantry, 7,224 cavalry, and 78 guns, he marched north to attack the Austrians, ignoring the increasing climate of anti-Napoleonic feeling in the country. On 4 April his forces won a minor victory at Modena, in northern central Italy over *Feldmarschalllleutnant* (FML) Baron Frederick von Bianchi. The Neapolitan commander in this action, General Filangieri, was killed.

Murat now tried to force the line of the River Po at Occhiobello, some 50km south of Venice, on 7 April, but was defeated. The Austrians had lost only 22 killed in this action, but the effects of the reverse on the brittle morale of Murat's officers and men was considerable. His officers included many Frenchmen and Poles and these two factions were at daggers-drawn and riven with dissent. The men of his army had no interest in the campaign at all and his army began to melt away. News then arrived of Britain's declaration of war against him; Murat was forced to order a withdrawal to the south. On 10 April the Neapolitan garrison of Carpi, just north of Modena was attacked by the Austrians and fled. Murat withdrew to Ravenna, near the eastern coast of the Italian peninsula, then to Cesenatico (clash on 23 April, which the Austrians won), Pesaro (28 April, another Austrian victory), Scapezzano (another Austrian victory on 1 May) and finally to Tolentino, halfway down Italy and 50km from the eastern coast, where, on 3 May, a decisive battle was fought.

Feldmarschalllleutnant (FML) Baron Frederick von Bianchi commanded the Austrian force detached to stop Murat's Neapolitans. On 30 April, Bianchi's Austrians reached Tolentino, aiming to block Murat's withdrawal to the south. At this point, Murat's army was at Macerata, 15km away to the north-east and approaching Tolentino, aiming to go to Foligno and on to the south.

Bianchi commanded 12 battalions, 10 squadrons and four batteries of artillery, totalling just under 11,000 men and 28 guns. Murat had 15,000 infantry, 2,000 cavalry and 35 guns. Bianchi knew that the odds were against him, but resolved to make a stand. The town of Tolentino was surrounded by its medieval walls and blocked the valley of the River Chienti, along which valley the road from Macerata to Foligno ran. This is now Route SS 77. Just east of Tolentino, this road runs in a narrow corridor, along the northern bank of the River Chienti. To the north of the Chienti was a ridge of gently rolling hills, running east to west and bounded on the north again by the River Potenza. A similar ridge ran parallel to this, immediately south of the River Chienti.

Each commander was well informed as to the other's forces. Murat issued an Order of the Day on 29 April: 'The moment we have waited so long for has come. 'This retreat was just a ruse; our victory over the Austrians is assured and will be an easy one.' Bianchi knew that he would be isolated and alone for the next few days and would have to face Murat's superior force on his own, but his position was a good one and he decided to stand because help was on its way, in the form of FML von Neipperg's division. He set Tolentino into a state of defence and deployed the main body of his troops north of the Chienti and into the hills towards the River Potenza. He sent his baggage train off to Serravalle and Belforte, 8km to the south-west.

On 1 May, Murat's main body was in Macerata, 12km north-east of Tolentino; next day, they advanced and pushed the Austrian patrols back towards Tolentino. There was an initial clash at Sforzacosta, some 10km from Tolentino. Murat's force was now increased by the arrival of part of General Lecchi's division and one of General Carascola's brigades; he now commanded 22,000 infantry, 3,500 cavalry and 35 guns – see Appendix for detailed order-of-battle..

Murat's army advanced in three columns, of which he personally commanded that in the centre. It consisted of the Royal Guard and a brigade of Carascola's division. The cavalry and the artillery were to advance along the valley of the Chienti, to the north of that river. One of Lecchi's brigades was sent south of the Chienti, to threaten Tolentino from the south, while Lieutenant-General Ambrosio was to advance on the northern flank. Murat's main column set off early on the morning of 2 May. The Austrian outposts, under Generalmajor von Starhemberg, fell back before them, without offering serious opposition, and were taken up by FML Mohr's division. A stiff combat developed in the hills of the northern flank, while south of the River Chienti, the Neapolitans pushed the small Austrian flank guards back on their main position before Tolentino.

In the Austrian line, the northern flank was held by Major-General Senitzer's division of 5 battalions and two squadrons of dragoons. FML Mohr commanded the centre and the southern flank, with brigades under von Starhemberg and von Taxis. The reserve was on the road to Osteria del Arancia. Although Murat's troops fought hard and well that day, they could not break through the Austrian line and the day's fighting ended in a stalemate at Tolentino, although other Austrian forces were making their way swiftly to support Bianchi.

Early on 3 May, Murat renewed the assault along the main road; Starhemberg fell back from Arancia and Guiboli onto FML von Mohr's division, who had occupied the western side of the steep valley of Cassone. Meanwhile, Ambrosio pushed the Austrians out of Vedova and Gallieso, to the east of Cassone. Murat decided to take Cassone and ordered his guard to assault the place. The place changed hands repeatedly before the Neapolitan superior numbers ensured that it remained in their hands. Now Murat ordered his troops to take the heights across the valley of Cassone, the key to the northern flank of the battlefield.

On the southern flank of the field, south of the River Chienti, the outnumbered Austrians fell back before General Lecchi's men, through Urbisaglia and Perindo to Vamocio, which they held against all attacks.

The key to the battle was on the northern flank, about the village of Madia. Here, the Neapolitans advanced out of Gallieso in four large squares, containing about 8-9,000 men. This is a most odd formation to adopt, as square was infantry's usual response to being threatened by large forces of enemy cavalry in open ground and the Austrians had only 10 squadrons in all. At about midday, a battery of Austrian artillery under Captain Kunerth, arrived on the field and opened up on the squares, which staggered to a halt. Bianchi seized the moment and attacked the leading square with IR Chasteler and two squadrons of the Toscana Dragoons. The effect was dramatic; the squares wavered, broke and fled back towards Gallieso. Seeing this, FML Mohr also advanced, threw the Neapolitans out of Cassone and over the valley. At this point, the leading column of Generalmajor von Echhardt appeared in the north, across the Potenza bridge at Molini at the same time that Murat heard that FML von Neipperg's column was also closing in on his rear. His resolve crumbled, as did his army; they fell back in the gathering darkness to the east. Murat spent the night in Macerata; next day he moved on eastwards to Fermo, in a swampy area near the coast.

Early on the morning of 4 May, Bianchi set off in pursuit, surprised the Neapolitans in their camps around Macerata and Sforzacosta and drove them off in disorder. Their army melted into a leaderless mob and fled to Fermo. Bianchi halted the chase, so as not to become engulfed in the swamps.

The Austrians at Tolentino, had lost 210 killed, 457 wounded and 143 missing. Murat's army lost 1,700 killed and wounded, 2,400 captured and a gun. The retreat to the south continued; the final outcome now inevitable. The last action in the campaign – a minor scuffle – was fought on 17 May at Mignano, 80km north of Naples, where 6,000 Neapolitan interior security troops under Macdonald, the Neapolitan Minister of War, were easily scared into fleeing the field by some 2,200 Austrian troops under FML Graf von Nugent. There were extremely few casualties. Peace negotiations began on 20 May. Murat fled to Corsica. Ferdinand IV of Sicily was rapidly restored to the throne of Naples, but Murat's colourful story was not yet over.

Joachim Murat, once scornfully dubbed 'King of the Cossacks!' by Napoleon in 1812, sometime King of Naples, was arrested on 8 October 1815 in Pizzo, on the coast of the toe of Italy, when he rashly attempted to land in his old kingdom and to recover it by the force of his personality. He was discovered, arrested and tried; the tribunal, after consultation, declared:

> That Joachim Murat, having by the fate of arms returned to the private station whence he sprung, had rashly landed in the Neapolitan dominions with twenty-eight followers, no longer relying upon war, but upon tumults and rioting; that he had excited the people to rebellion; that he had offended the rightful King; that he had attempted to throw the kingdom of Naples and the whole of Italy into confusion; and that therefore, as a public enemy, he was condemned to die, by authority of the law of the Decennium, which was still in vigour.

This very law, was one which Murat himself had passed seven years before. On 13 October 1815, he was led out to face his execution, in a little courtyard of his castle prison, where he found a party of soldiers – the firing squad. He remained utterly calm, and refused a blindfold. He then called out to the soldiers, 'Spare my face — aim at the heart!' No sooner had he uttered these words than the party fired, and he fell dead. In 1816, following his death, , the formal union of the Kingdom of Naples with the Kingdom of Sicily into the new Kingdom of the Two Sicilies took place.

Murat left two sons and two daughters. The eldest son, Napoléon-Achille (1801–1847), went to the United States of America in 1821, became an American citizen and died in Florida. The younger son, Napoléon-Lucien-Charles (1803–1878) also went to the United States, in 1825, but returned to France in 1848 and was recognized as a prince of the Second Empire by Napoleon III with the title of Prince Murat. From him descended the princely house of Murat, which survived into the 20th century

Generalities Concerning Uniforms

The uniforms of the various arms of service are detailed in the introductions to the various chapters. However, some generalities apply across the army as a whole, pertaining in particular to distinction between ranks. The national cockade was amaranthe (magenta) within white. The weaponry for the army was either imported from France or manufactured to French designs within the kingdom.

Under Joseph and Murat, the French system of badges of military rank and company distinction were introduced. For NCOs, these were worn on the sleeves. If the cuffs were round or had flaps, they consisted of straight, diagonal bars, lifting to the rear; if the cuffs were pointed, they were in the form of chevrons, point uppermost.

- Corporal: two red bars/chevrons.
- Corporal Quartermaster: two red bars/chevrons over the cuff and a further red bar on the upper left arm.
- Sergeant: one gold bar/chevron on red backing.
- Sergeant-Major: two gold bars on red.
- Adjudant Sous-Officier (Chief Warrant Officer): gold epaulettes with two red stripes along the straps and red fringes mixed into the gold on both shoulders, red and gold sword strap and tassel.

Officers of all regiments except hussars wore epaulettes in the button colour according to rank; company officers wore thin silk fringes to the epaulette on the left shoulder and their sword strap had thin silk fringes. Field officers (major and above) wore heavy bullion fringes to epaulettes and sword strap.

- Second lieutenant: two red stripes along the epaulette straps.
- Lieutenant; one red stripe along the epaulette strap.
- Captain: plain straps.
- Chef de Bataillon: heavy fringes to the left shoulder, no fringes to the right shoulder.
- Major: epaulette straps in the opposite colour to the buttons, fringes in the button colour.
- Colonel: heavy fringes, to both epaulettes, in the button colour.

Hussar officers wore chevrons over their cuffs in the button colour and also had lace in the button colour to the fronts of their thighs.

2

Staff Officers and Aides-de-Camp

There were two ranks of general officer in the Neapolitan service, Tenente Generale and Maresciallo di Campo. These equated to the contemporary French Général de Division and Général de Brigade, although Boisselier – who throughout this series renders Neapolitan ranks into French – gives a more literal equivalent. Uniform was a bicorn with cockade, gold loop and button, gold lace edging and white feather trim; dark blue tunic and britches with crimson collar and cuffs. Tunic and britches were lavishly decorated with lace, and a crimson and silver waist sash was worn. General staff officers were similarly-attired but with crimson britches and a light blue tunic collar.

STAFF OFFICERS AND AIDES-DE-CAMP

Lieutenant Général 1811
This general officer wears the star and light blue sash of the Royal Order of the Two Sicilies, founded on 24 February 1808 by King Joseph. His rank is shown by the white feather edging to his hat, his scimitar and the gold embroidery to tunic and breeches, as well as his gold epaulettes and scimitar strap.
Plate 249781. Source: Museum of San Martino.

MURAT'S ARMY

Aide-de-Camp du Roi, Maréchal-de-Camp, Grande Uniforme 1812-1813
Not only is his uniform lavishly decorated with gold braid, even the harness of his horse seems to be similarly treated. Interestingly enough, the crowned royal cipher in the rear corner of the shabraque is shown as `JN`, which was King Joseph`s cipher; that of Joachim Murat was just the crowned `J`.
Plate 249778. Source: Museum of San Martino.

STAFF OFFICERS AND AIDES-DE-CAMP

Chef d'Escadron, Aide-de-Camp du Roi Joachim Murat 1812
This most impracticable uniform must have been a nightmare to maintain. It is not clear if the red facings and sabretache centre are meant to be in the royal amaranthe, but the cipher is correct for Murat, whose hand and flamboyant tastes may clearly be seen in this glittering, extravagantly expensive and hopelessly impractical hussar-finery, which reeks of the comic opera.
Plate 249824. Source: Museum of San Martino.

MURAT'S ARMY

Aide de Camp 1812
It was customary in Napoleonic armies of this period to deck out ADCs on the general staff rather like peacocks and they often wielded the power of the ranks of their bosses, which much increased their already considerable egos. This costume is surprisingly modest. The royal cipher on the breastplate of the horse is `J`, while that in the rear corner of the shabraque is `N`; this is an impossible combination. Plate 249776. Source: Museum of San Martino.

STAFF OFFICERS AND AIDES-DE-CAMP

Capitaine de l'Etat Major de l'Armée, 1812-1813
The hussar-style waistcoat and breeches lend an air of the dashing cavalryman to this figure
and the braids on his collar give a hint of the status of the Royal Guard as well.
Plate 249777. Source: Museum of San Martino.

MURAT'S ARMY

Capitaine Adjutant du Place, 1812-1813
The officers `du Place` were members of the staffs of garrisons, who arranged matters of supply, accommodation, discipline, rations and forage for passing military regiments. His gorget bears the crowned royal cipher `JN` and is thus wrong for King Joachim Murat.
Plate 249870. Source: Museum of San Martino.

STAFF OFFICERS AND AIDES-DE-CAMP

Capitaine, Gouvernement de Naples, 1812
The green uniform with amaranthe facings seems a rather unusual choice of colour scheme for a sedentary official. The badges on his shako plate and gorget seem to be grenades, which are equally surprising.
Plate 249868. Source: Museum of San Martino.

3
The Royal Guard

In 1806 the cavalry of the guard consisted of one regiment of *Veliti a Cavallo*, of two squadrons, each of two companies. In 1809 a squadron of *Guardia d'Onore* was been added: This unit was formed of the two squadrons of the Lancers of Berg, which Murat brought with him when he accepted the throne of Naples. In 1813 the *Veliti a Cavallo* were converted into a regiment of hussars (*Ussaro*). There were now also regiments of Cuirassiers (*Corazzieri*), raised in late 1813, Chevaulegers, and Chevaulegers-Lanciers so that in the 1815 campaign the Guard Cavalry could muster a whole division.

Infantry of the Guard included one regiment of Grenadiers (*Granatieri*) and one of Voltigeurs (*Volteggiatori*). Each had two four-company battalions, plus a depot company. By 1809 they had been joined by two regiments of Velites (*Veliti*), of the same establishment as the grenadiers, a one-battalion regiment of Marine Infantry (*Marino della Guardia Real*). As of 1813, the colours of the Royal Guard infantry regiments were square, light blue with a chequered magenta and white frame. The regimental inscription was painted in gold. The inscription for the grenadiers read: GIOACCHINO NAPOLEONE / AL REGIMENTO / DI GRANATIERI A PIEDI / DELLA GUARDIA REALE. There was a light blue cravat, with crowned royal cipher in gold, a strip of magenta and white dicing and golden fringes at either end. The ends of the cravat reached to about three-quarters of the way down the colour. The finial was a prancing gold charger on a plinth.

By 1809 the Guard Artillery one battery each of foot and horse artillery, each with a train company. The foot battery had six 8-pounder cannon and two howitzers, the horse battery had four 4-pounder guns and two howitzers, all of the French Gribeauval design. There was also a battalion of veterans of the guard.

THE ROYAL GUARD

Compagnie de Gardes du Corps, 1812
This trooper is in parade dress, as shown by his plume and the ornate bandolier, which echoes details of the equipment worn by the Spanish royal guards. The crowned royal cipher is correct for Murat.
Plate 249774. Source: Museum of San Martino.

MURAT'S ARMY

Compagnie de Gardes du Corps, Petit Tenue, 1812
When Murat left the Grand Duchy of Berg to assume the Neapolitan throne, many members of the 1st Regiment of the Lancers of Berg accompanied him and became his Garde du Corps. We see echoes of that lancer uniform here, but the colour scheme bears no relation to that original unit. The royal cipher on the czapka plate is 'JN' which relates to King Joseph, not to Murat.
Plate 249775. Source: Museum of San Martino.

THE ROYAL GUARD

Colonel, Grenadiers de la Garde Royale, 1812
The costume reflects the national amaranth together with the dark blue tunic and is dripping with gold braid and tassels. The white plume appears to be a single feather, which must be wrong; it would have been a cut feather plume.
Plate 249817. Source: Museum of San Martino.

MURAT'S ARMY

Grenadier du Regt. de Grenadiers de la Garde Royale 1812
This figure is of a private in parade order, complete with pack. Note that the grenadier fitments are red, whilst the facings are amaranthe.
Plate 249818. Source: Museum of San Martino.

THE ROYAL GUARD

Officier de Voltigeurs de la Garde Royale 1815
The meaning of the diagonal stripes around the shako is unclear. From the epaulettes and the ring of gold embroidery around the top of the shako, this man would seem to be a *Chef de Bataillon*. The gold, tasselled lace on the pointed cuffs is most unconventional.
Plate 249812. Source: Museum of San Martino.

MURAT'S ARMY

Voltigeur de la Garde Royale 1815
Once again, the national amaranthe features as the facing colour and the shako bears the odd diagonal stripes. The French-style company badges include a yellow collar, the green pompon and the green and yellow epaulettes. His sabre strap would also be green.
Plate 249809. Source: Museum of San Martino.

THE ROYAL GUARD

Officier Superieur des Cuirassiers de la Garde Royale 1812-1813.
The colour scheme is a dark blue tunic and horse furniture, amaranthe facings and silver buttons and lace. The bearskin harks back to the horse grenadiers of Napoleon's Imperial Guard, as does the grenade badge in the corner of the square, heavy cavalry shabraque. The horses of this regiment would have been large, about 16 hands high.
Plate 249772. Source: Museum of San Martino.

MURAT'S ARMY

Cuirassiers de la Garde Royale, Grande Tenue 1812-1813
The buff and white bandolier and belt, with the grenade badge on the buckle plate were also worn by the Elite
Gendarmes of Napoleon's Imperial Guard. Just what makes this 'grande tenue' is not immediately clear.
Plate 249773. Source: Museum of San Martino.

THE ROYAL GUARD

Velite de la Garde Royale, Grande Tenue 1807
This man is an Adjudant Sous-Officier, a first-class warrant officer, as shown by his red and gold epaulettes and sword strap. He also wears officer-style gold trim to his bicorn.
Plate 249796. Source: *Décrets et lois du Royaume de Naples*.

MURAT'S ARMY

Major de 1er Regt. de Vélites de la Garde Royale 1812
His rank is shown by the silver straps to his gold-fringed epaulettes; he is in parade dress, complete with gilt gorget with silver crest. Murat's love of gilt, braid, and tassels sadly lends an air of the comic opera to the costume.
Plate 249815. Source: Museum of San Martino.

THE ROYAL GUARD

Sergent Major du 1er. Regt. de Vélites de la Garde Royale
No date is given, but 1812 would be a safe bet. The fittings of his rank are the gold and green bearskin cords, epaulettes and sabre strap and the gold on red bars on his forearms. On another plate of this regiment, Boisselier shows an eagle badge on the cap plate.
Plate 249816. Source: Museum of San Martino.

MURAT'S ARMY

1er Regt. de Vélites de la Garde Royale, Grande Tenue 1813
Boisselier has dated this sketch of a member of the regiment's voltiguer company to the 16 November 1813; the man is in parade dress and the company badges comply with those of the French army, including the green plume and sabre strap and the green and yellow epaulettes.
Plate 249813. Source: *Ordonnances et Décrets du Royaume de Naples.*

THE ROYAL GUARD

2e Regt. de Vélites de la Garde Royale, Chef de Bataillon 1812-1813
This officer is in parade dress, complete with cane. His gilt gorget shows that he is on
duty with troops. The 1st Regiment had red facings, the 2nd had amaranthe.
Plate 249814. Source: Museum of San Martino.

MURAT'S ARMY

2e Regt. de Vélites de la Garde Royale, 1812-1813
It is interesting to note that amaranthe seems to have replaced red on the half-moons of his epaulettes. He is in the light company, as shown by the green plume, sabre strap and green and amaranthe epaulettes. He also wears the guards' two-colour bandoliers.
Plate 249811. Source: Museum of San Martino.

THE ROYAL GUARD

Velite à Cheval de la Garde Royale 1807
'Velites' were lightly armed soldiers in the Roman army in antiquity, the name being revived by Napoleon and clearly borrowed by Joseph and Murat. Following the French scheme, the very definite red stripes along the epaulette straps and the red tassels mixed into the epaulette fringes, show that we are dealing here with an adjudant sous-officier, the senior non-commissioned rank of chief warrant officer. The golden threads in the sword strap confirm this. Note his red waist belt edged in gold.
Plate 249797. Source: Museum of San Martino.

MURAT'S ARMY

Hussards de la Garde Royale, Grande Tenue 1812
Caption notwithstanding, this plate in fact portrays the uniform adopted by the Velites à Cheval from 1809 onwards when the original uniform was replaced by hussar-style dress. The full dress reflects the national colours of amaranthe and white. Unusually for hussars, the figure wears gauntlets and they even have black cuffs.
Plate 249821. Source: Museum of San Martino.

THE ROYAL GUARD

Hussards de la Garde Royale, Grande Tenue November 1813
After the regiment was formally converted to hussars in 1813, the gaudy old costume gave way to the much more sober green and red seen on this trooper here. The crowned cipher on the sabretache, 'J', is correct for Murat.
Plate 249822. Source: *Ordonnances et Decrets du Royaume de Naples*.

MURAT'S ARMY

Hussards de la Garde Royale, Tenue de Campagne 1813
In campaign dress, the red breeches give way to green overalls. The harness is plain black leather with minimal decoration.
Plate 249819. Source: *Ordonnances et Décrets du Royaume de Naples.*

THE ROYAL GUARD

Chevaulegers de la Garde Royale, Capitaine, Grande Tenue 1812
We see here a uniform which links directly back to the Lancers of Berg, who followed Murat to Naples to form this elite unit. The czapka plate however, bears the crowned royal cipher 'JN', which relates to King Joseph Napoleon in the years 1806-1808.
Plate 249825. Source: Museum of San Martino.

MURAT'S ARMY

Chevaulegers de la Garde Royale, Petit Uniforme 1812
The uniform for daily duties was much more practical than the full dress outfit. We also see here the crowned cipher 'J', which – correctly – agrees with the date of 1812.
Plate 249823. Source: Museum of San Martino.

THE ROYAL GUARD

Chevaulegers de la Garde Royale, Grande Tenue 1813
We see that 'grande tenue' has changed radically since 1812. Despite all the apparent glamour, this figure is only a trooper. Once again, the czapka plate shows the cipher 'JN' for King Joseph, instead of the correct 'J'. Plate 249779. Source: *Ordonnances et Decrets du Royaume de Naples*.

MURAT'S ARMY

Officier de Lanciers, Grande Tenue, 1812
Boisselier is even more vague than usual with his caption for this figure, but this would seem to be a representation of the Chevauleger-Lancier Regiment of the Royal Guard. The plume appears to be composed of greenish-black cock's tail feathers, and it seems that even junior officers had the band of embroidery to the top of the shako. The royal ciphers (JN) on shako and shabraque are uncrowned and relate to King Joseph Napoleon of 1806-1808.
Plate 249852. Source: Museum of San Martino.

THE ROYAL GUARD

Lancier, Grande Tenue 1812
Again, lack of similarity with the known dress of line cavalry regiments leaves us with the inference that this is a trooper of the Guard Chevauleger-Lanciers. The royal ciphers (JN) relate to the period 1806-1808, however, which is dubious. Plate 249850. Source: Museum of San Martino.

MURAT'S ARMY

Artillerie à Cheval de la Garde Royale, Petite Tenue, 1812
This is the undress, or everyday uniform and is very like that of the French Imperial Guard, The facings, epaulette fringes, busby bag and piping seem to be amaranthe in colour, whereas the plume and pompon are red.
Plate 249820. Source: Museum of San Martino.

4

The Line Cavalry

In 1806 there were two regiments of Chasseurs à Cheval (*Cacciatori a Cavallo*), each of three field squadrons, each of two companies, and a depot squadron. On 25 December 1810 the Chevauleger (*Cavalleggieri*) Regiment was raised. In March 1813 the two regiments of Chasseurs became the 1st and 2nd Chevaulegers, the existing Chevauleger Regiment was given the number 3, and a new 4th Regiment was raised. These re-designations were accompanied by changes to uniform and the adoption of lances, but the process was not a straightforward one as the plates and their captions indicate.

The cavalry standards for this period were square, having an internal frame of a double row of amaranthe and white dicing, within which was the unit title. All within a circular gold wreath of oak and laurel leaves and under a crown, surmounting the cipher 'GN'. The other side of the standard would have the crowned small crest of Naples, within the diced border.

Standard of the 1st Regiment of Cacciatore a Cavallo
The cloth is light blue, with amaranthe and white dicing, the inscription and the crest are painted on in gold. (Author's collection)

MURAT'S ARMY

1er Regt. Chevaulegers, Officier, Petite Tenue 1812-1813
This costume would be referred to in English as 'undress uniform' and would be worn for everyday duties. It is not clear what the badges of the picker equipment on the black bandolier are, but this man is a junior officer. As in the French army, the elite company wore fur colpacks with a grenade badge pierced with the regimental number and a bag in the facing colour.
Plate 249808. Source: Museum of San Martino.

THE LINE CAVALRY

1er Regt. Chevaulegers, Grande Tenue 1812-1815
It was quite usual for nations to convert light cavalry regiments to lancers at this point, although Britain did not follow suit until after the Napoleonic wars. Only the front rank of the regiment would have been equipped with lances, the second rank having sabres and carbines. The lance pennon would seem to have been in the regimental facing colour over white, rather than in amaranthe and white. His rhombic, brass cap plate bears just the regimental numeral '1'.
Plate 249805. Source: Museum of San Martino.

MURAT'S ARMY

2e Regt. Chevaulegers, Officier, Petite Tenue 1813
Caption notwithstanding, this is the old green chasseur uniform, which this regiment – being on active service in Germany – continued to wear for some time after conversion to chevaulegers. This officer is shown in *petite tenue* or everyday dress. His plain black sabretache is unusual in bearing not even a crowned cipher. Presumably the parade version would be decorated with the royal cipher.
Plate 249806. Source: Museum of San Martino.

THE LINE CAVALRY

2e Regt. Chevaulegers, Sous-officier, Cie. d'Elite 1813
The badges of rank are the silver chevrons (the button colour) above the cuff, indicating the rank of sergeant; elite company status is shown by the red epaulettes and pompon. He wears *petite tenue*; note the brass grenade on the busby. Again, this is the old chasseur uniform.
Plate 249803. Source: Museum of San Martino.

MURAT'S ARMY

2e Regt. Chevaulegers 1814

There has been a complete change of uniform from the previous year; the shako plate bears the regimental numeral. The facings seem to be amaranthe; the figure wears *petite tenue*, with leather reinforcing to the overalls. In addition to the plates in this series, Boisselier painted a plate of three members of the 2nd Chevaulegers Regiment in the 1814-1815 period, showing a trumpeter, an adjudant sous-officier, and a chef d'escadron, all in light blue uniforms, with amaranthe facings and white buttons, The trumpeter holds a brass trumpet with a light blue trumpet banner, edged in silver and amaranthe fringes and bearing the small crest of Naples, on an ermine coat surmounted by the crown. Plate 249804. Source: From a collection of plates on the uniforms of the Neapolitan army.

THE LINE CAVALRY

3e Regt. Chevaulegers, Chef d'Escadron, 1813
This officer wears *petite tenue*, with lemon yellow facings and white buttons
Plate 249801. Source: Museum of San Martino.

MURAT'S ARMY

3e Regt. Chevaulegers, Sappeur, Grande Tenue 1812-1813
What constitutes 'full dress' seems to have changed, so that overalls have been promoted from *petite tenue*. As a sapper, he wears a full beard and has the red grenade badge on his upper left arm and the grenadier's red epaulettes. The sapper badges were usually worn on both arms. Full dress normally includes a plume.
Plate 249802. The source is unclear.

THE LINE CAVALRY

4e Regt. Chevaulegers, Grande Tenue 1812-1813
That this modestly dressed cavalryman is wearing full dress is even more questionable, when one notices the brass mess tin, fastened on top of his valise. Full dress usually includes a plume and shako cords; this looks very much like *petite tenue*. The sheepskin saddle cover was also usually worn on campaign.
Plate 249800. Source: Museum of San Martino.

5

The Line Infantry

In 1806 there were two regiments each of two field battalions, each of nine companies: 1 grenadier, 1 of voltigeurs, 7 of fusiliers and a depot battalion of four fusilier companies. By 1809 there were seven line regiments, each of three field battalions, now on the standard French scale of one grenadier, one light and four centre companies. By 1812 there were eight regiments of line infantry, eventually rising to twelve by 1814.

The initial uniforms of the line regiments were white coats without flaps to the cuffs and with bicorne hats. The skirts of the coat reached to the back of the knee. In 1809 the coat skirts of the men were shortened by about three inches. Those of the officers remained so long, that they reached to the back of the knee. The 1st Regiment wore its light blue facings on collar, cuffs, lapels and piping to the white shoulder straps, pockets and the white turnbacks, the 2nd Regiment initially also had light blue lapels, cuffs and piping, with a white collar, piped light blue. This later changed to scarlet facings. The cuffs initially had two buttons; later this changed to three. Buttons were brass and bore the regimental number within a French ring. The fatigue cap was white (having been made up from old jackets), piped in the facing colour. Belts and breeches were also white. Badges of rank and inter-company distinctions were of the French models. Drummers wore white chevrons on their sleeves, being piped in dark blue and bearing red diamonds along their length. They also had swallows nests in the facing colour to the tops of their sleeves. From 1811 onwards, this lace became crimson with white checks and in addition to the decoration described above, they also wore seven chevrons of this tape, point up, on each sleeve.

In 1809 the colour of the new line infantry tunic changed to blue and the grenadiers now wore plain bearskin bonnets with a red top patch bearing a yellow grenade and red grenades on their turnbacks. They wore red epaulettes and red plumes in parade dress. The light companies adopted yellow collars and had yellow hunting horns on their turnbacks. Voltigeurs had yellow collars, and green epaulettes with yellow crescents. Turnback emblems were white grenades, yellow hunting horns and, for the fusilier companies white, 5-pointed stars, white, heart-shaped patches or yellow crowns.

In 1809 French-style shakos began to be issued; they had a brass, shield-shaped front plate For grenadiers the plate bore a flaming grenade bearing the regimental number. They also wore a red pompon. Voltigeurs' plates had a grenade over a hunting horn, or the crowned cipher 'J' and a yellow pompon. The fusilier companies wore pompons on the shakos in the following colours: 1st Company – green, 2nd – sky blue; 3rd – orange; 4th – violet. The voltigeur company wore green pompons and yellow-over-green plumes and cords in full dress.

In 1811 new white uniforms were issued, they were of the French style, with facings worn on the collar, lapels, shoulder straps, cuffs and cuff flaps, all these parts being piped white. The tunic skirts were now shorter than before for the men; the skirts of officers' tunics still reached to the back of the knee.

Regimental titles and uniform distinctions up until 1811 were as follows:

1st Regiment 'del Re' Raised in 1806; white coat, sky blue facings; plain round cuffs.

2nd Regiment 'della Regina' Raised in 1806; white coat, light red facings; plain round cuffs.

3rd Regiment 'del Principe Real' Raised in 1809; dark blue coat, black facings; flaps to the cuffs.

4th Regiment 'Real Sannita' Raised in 1809; dark blue coat, amaranth facings; flaps to the cuffs.

5th Regiment 'Real Calabria' Raised in 1809; dark blue coat, orange facings; flaps to the cuffs.

6th Regiment 'Napoli' Raised in 1810 from the Naples City Guard; sky blue coat, crimson facings; flaps to the cuffs.

7th Regiment 'Real Africano' In 1803, Negroes and mulattos who had immigrated to France from the West Indies and Saint-Domingue were grouped together as a battalion designated the *Pionniers Noirs*. When the Kingdom of Naples was established in 1806, these 'black pioneers' were transferred into the service of the new state on 14 August, and were increased to regimental strength and designated the 7th Regiment in 1810. The regiment continued to wear its French uniform of light brown coat, scarlet facings; plain round cuffs.

THE LINE INFANTRY

After the issue of new uniforms in 1811, and for units raised thereafter, titles and uniform distinctions were as follows:

1st Regiment 'del Re' sky blue facings, pointed cuffs.

2nd Regiment 'della Regina' light red facings, pointed cuffs.

3rd Regiment 'del Principe Real' black facings, pointed cuffs.

4th Regiment 'Real Sannita' amaranthe facings, pointed cuffs.

5th Regiment 'Real Calabria' orange facings, pointed cuffs.

6th Regiment 'di Napoli' orange facings, pointed cuffs.

7th Regiment 'Real Africano' yellow facings, pointed cuffs.

8th Regiment 'Principe Luciano' pink facings, pointed cuffs.

9th Regiment light blue facings, pointed cuffs.

10th Regiment blue facings; flaps to the cuffs. Raised in 1814.

11th Regiment amaranthe facings; flaps to the cuffs. Raised in 1814.

12th Regiment 'della Marca' green facings; flaps to the cuffs. Raised on 29 June 1814.

It seems that only the battalions of the 1st through 4th Line and the 1st and 2nd Light Regiments (see next chapter) received the 1806 pattern colours, issued on a scale of one to each battalion. These were much akin to their contemporary French equivalents of the 1804 pattern, having a central white lozenge bearing the regimental title with the remaining corner triangles in red and black. Embroidery was silver. They were 80 cm square, mounted on black staves, with a brass ferrule and a plain iron spear-head shaped finial.

In 1810-11, new style colours were issued to all units, again, at a scale of one per battalion. There were two patterns; one for the guard and the other for the line, all – theoretically – measured 85 cm x 78 cm. The cloth was light blue, with an inset border of a double row of white and magenta checks; within this border, the gold crown over the royal cipher, over the gold regimental designation, within a wreath of laurel and oak leaves, tied with a gold ribbon.

The exceptions to this norm were the colours of the 5th Line regiment (captured by the Russians at the fall of Danzig in 1813) which measured 150 x 130 cm and that of the 6th Line, which had a crimson field. The 1811 pattern colours were carried on staves painted with white and amaranth spirals and most regiments had a light blue cravat, with gold fringes and sometimes a diced border, as on the colours, tied below the finial. The 5th Line had two cravats, one green and one violet: the 6th Line also had two cravats, both white with gold fringes. The cords were of gold and the plain, iron finial had been replaced by the gilt prancing horse of Naples on the capital of a Corinthian column.

MURAT'S ARMY

1er Regt. d'Infanterie de Ligne, Capitaine 1812
The shako plate bears the usual, dubious, uncrowned royal cipher ('JN') of King Joseph and the gilt gorget seems to bear a hunting horn, but it might well be something else. This officer wears *petite tenue*. Note the amaranthe threads in the tassel of his golden sword strap.
Plate 249851. Source: Museum of San Martino.

THE LINE INFANTRY

2e Regt. d'Infanterie de Ligne, Fusilier, Grande Tenue 1812
As previously stated, full dress usually included a plume and shako cords, which are missing here. Again, the royal cipher on the shako plate is 'JN', which relates to King Joseph, and the crown is missing.
Plate 249848. Source: Museum of San Martino.

MURAT'S ARMY

3e Regt. d'Infanterie de Ligne, Grenadier, Grande Tenue 1812
White uniforms were ordered for all line infantry regiments in 1811, although the existing old garments would have continued to be worn until they needed replacement. He wears the cords and plume required for full dress.
Plate 249849. Source: Museum of San Martino.

THE LINE INFANTRY

4e Regt. d'Infanterie de Ligne, Voltigeur, Grande Tenue 1812
As is usual, the shako has neither the plume nor the cords, which one normally associates with full dress. The shako plate bears a hunting horn and the pompon is yellow, but one would expect the collar of the tunic also to be yellow. He carries no sabre, which – for an elite company – is very unusual.
Plate 249846. Source: Museum of San Martino.

MURAT'S ARMY

4e Regt. d'Infanterie de Ligne, Artillerie Régimentaire 2 April 1813
Regimental artillery companies would have two guns apiece, plus the attached limbers, ammunition wagons, horse teams and drivers. In view of the date of the order creating them, it is extremely doubtful if any were actually formed. This figure is in marching order; he wears a grenade shako plate and red epaulettes, pompon and sabre strap; his facings seem to be amaranthe, the buttons, brass. Presumably, the grenade badge and the grenadier epaulettes are the mark of the regimental gunners.
Plate 249847. Source: *Décrets et lois du Royaume de Naples*.

THE LINE INFANTRY

5e Regt. d'Infanterie de Ligne, Grenadier, Grande Tenue 1812
This man wears the red plume and cords to his bearskin, which go to make up 'full dress'. The green tassel of his fatigue cap may just be seen, dangling from under his cartridge pouch, where it was carried, rolled up.
Plate 249844. Source: Museum of San Martino.

MURAT'S ARMY

5e Regt. d'Infanterie de Ligne, Sappeur, Grande Tenue 1812
Sappers carried not only axes, but also saws and other tools, with which to dismantle buildings and obstacles in the field and also to build bridges and other, defensive, structures as required. They did not shave, in recognition of the fact that their duties often took them away from the usual camp-site facilities.
Plate 249845. Source: Museum of San Martino.

THE LINE INFANTRY

6e Regt. d'Infanterie de Ligne, Porte Drapeau 1812
The officer who carried the regimental colours was usually a junior lieutenant. The shako plate cipher – uncrowned – is plainly 'JN', which is correct for Joseph Napoleon in the years 1806-1808, but incorrect for Joachim Murat in 1812. Plate 249842. Source: Museum of San Martino.

MURAT'S ARMY

7e Regt. d'Infanterie de Ligne, Officier de Grenadiers 1812
Boisselier included the note: 'Ex Royal Africain', relating to the title of the unit in French service.
It is impossible to decipher what the badge on the gilt gorget is supposed to be.
Plate 249843. Source: Museum of San Martino.

THE LINE INFANTRY

8e Regt. d'Infanterie de Ligne, Officier de Voltigeurs 1812
The shako plate bears a crowned hunting horn, as does the gilt gorget; the pink facings were a strange choice. The yellow collar and pompon are the badges of the light company.
Plate 249840. Source: Museum of San Martino.

MURAT'S ARMY

9e Regt. d'Infanterie de Ligne, Adjudant-Major 1812-1813
Boisselier shows some figures in the 1813-1814 period with patches in the facing colour to the fronts of the collars and others without. This may be another uniform change, which did not get fully implemented, and the date at which the design of the collar of the tunic changed is not clear. At least, the designs of the shako plate and gorget – flaming grenades – are clear. This regiment was raised in 1812; note the cuff with flaps and buttons.
Plate 249841. Source: Museum of San Martino.

THE LINE INFANTRY

9e Regt. d'Infanterie de Ligne, Fusilier 1813
Again we see the modified collar, which seems to place the change of design in the early half of 1813. The shako plate design in merely an annoyingly confusing squiggle. This man wears marching order.
Plate 249838. Source: Museum of San Martino.

MURAT'S ARMY

10e Regt. d'Infanterie de Ligne, Officier de Grenadiers 1813
This company officer wears the cords and plume to his bearskin, which indicate that he is in full dress. His collar is of the 1813 pattern and his gorget bears a silver grenade.
Plate 249839. Source: Museum of San Martino.

THE LINE INFANTRY

11e Regt. d'Infanterie de Ligne, Officier de Fusiliers 1813
Boisselier has again inserted the uncrowned royal ciphers 'JN' onto shako plate and gorget, which is an anachronism, as in this year the cipher 'GN' was in use. The man is in *petite tenue* and wears the 1813 pattern collar.
Plate 249836. Source: Museum of San Martino.

MURAT'S ARMY

12e Regt. d'Infanterie de Ligne, Sous-officier de Fusiliers 1813
The single gold bar over the cuff shows that this man is a sergeant and the design of his collar is correct for the post-1813 period, but Colin Allen, a specialist in Neapolitan Napoleonic uniforms, is clear that the 12th was raised on 29 June 1814; has Boisselier been less than careful with yet another detail in the title of his painting?
Plate 249837. Source: Museum of San Martino.

6

The Light Infantry

In 1806 there was one regiment of light infantry of two field battalions and a depot battalion. Each field battalion had a *carabinieri* company (equivalent to the grenadiers of the line regiments), a light company of *volteggiatore* and seven companies of *cacciatore* (chasseurs). The depot battalion had just four companies of *cacciatore*. There was also the regiment *Real Corso* (Royal Corsican) which was organized as a light regiment. By 1809 there were three light regiments, including the *Real Corso*, each of three field battalions and a depot battalion.

By 1813 there were four light infantry regiments in the army and they wore blue uniforms with white buttons, which bore the regimental number within a hunting horn. Light infantry regiments had the same establishments as the line regiments, with three six-company battalions per regiment. In 1813 the regiment *Real Corso* became the 1st Light Infantry Regiment (with black facings) and the old 1st and 2nd became the 2nd and 3rd. The 2nd Regiment was raised in 1806 as the 1st, and had yellow facings. The 3rd Regiment was raised in 1809 as the 2nd, and had scarlet facings. A 4th Regiment was also raised in 1813 and had orange facings.

For details of colours, see the introduction to the previous chapter.

MURAT'S ARMY

1er Regt. d'Infanterie Légère, Lieutenant de Voltigeurs 1812
This is the old *Real Corso*, which became the 1st Light Infantry Regiment only in 1813. The silver shako plate bears a crowned hunting horn and the gorget just a horn.
Plate 249832. Source: Museum of San Martino.

THE LIGHT INFANTRY

1er Regt. d'Infanterie Légère, Carabinier 1812
Again, this is the old *Real Corso*. The figure is shown in grande tenue but the white cords to the bearskin seem to be questionable, as they were usually red.
Plate 249834. Source: Museum of San Martino.

MURAT'S ARMY

1er Regt. d'Infanterie Légère, Artillerie Régimentaire 2 April 1813
The regimental artillery companies seem to have worn red epaulettes but fusilier shakos as their uniform. As with their equivalents for the line infantry regiments, it seems unlikely that these companies were ever actually formed. Plate 249835. Source: *Ordonnances et Decrets du Royaume de Naples*.

THE LIGHT INFANTRY

2e Regt. d'Infanterie Légère, Carabinier 1812
As with the previous set of plates, Boisselier is using the 1813 numbering; in 1812, this unit would still have been numbered as the 1st Regiment. Again we see white cords to the bearskin, where red would be more conventional.
Plate 249830. Source: Museum of San Martino

MURAT'S ARMY

2e Regt. d'Infanterie Légère, Officier de Chasseurs 1812-1813
Boisselier has here omitted the crown from above the horn on the shako plate, which he was careful to include on his plate of an officer of the 1st Light Infantry Regiment.
Plate 249833. Source: Museum of San Martino.

THE LIGHT INFANTRY

3e Regt. d'Infanterie Légère, Officier de Carabiniers 1812
The scarlet facings confirm that Boisselier has again applied the 1813 numbering to what in 1812 would still have been the 2nd Regiment. The figure adheres to all the details that we find in other documentation.
Plate 249831. Source: Museum of San Martino.

MURAT'S ARMY

3e Regt. d'Infanterie Légère, Voltigeur 1812
The pompon, epaulettes and the yellow collar confirm the voltigeur status. The horn on the shako plate is shown under a crown, which is most probably correct. It is odd that this man carried no sabre, but wears a fusilier's pouch belt with integrated bayonet frog.
Plate 249828. Source: Museum of San Martino.

THE LIGHT INFANTRY

4e Regt. d'Infanterie Légère, Adjudant Sous-Officier 1812-1813
Note that that this man wears a gorget and carries a cane, but has no officer-pattern
sword knot. Interestingly, his shako plate and gorget bear grenades.
Plate 249829. Source: Museum of San Martino.

MURAT'S ARMY

4e Regt. d'Infanterie Légère, Chasseur 1812-1813
This is a very modest uniform. Note the unusual placing of the button at the lower end of the shoulder strap.
Plate 249826. Source: Museum of San Martino.

7

Technical Troops

In 1806 there was just one battery of field artillery, equipped with 6-pounder Austrian-pattern cannon. By the following year this had grown to a regiment of foot artillery, a battalion of train, a battalion of artificers and armourers, and a battalion of sappers and miners. By 1809 the field artillery had grown to four batteries, each equipped with six Gribeauval cannon and two howitzers. By 1812 there were 12 foot and two horse batteries. The horse batteries had four cannon and two howitzers each. Each field battery had its company of Artillery Train. The foot artillery wore dark blue uniforms of infantry cut, with red facings and yellow buttons. The horse artillery wore the uniforms of Chasseur à Cheval style in dark blue with red facings and yellow buttons.

There were also 18 companies of coastal defence artillery, two companies of artificers, one company of pontoniers, and five companies of sappers and miners. The all-officer corps of engineers wore uniforms of artillery style with black facings and silver buttons. Boisselier seems not to have painted these units.

MURAT'S ARMY

Train d'Artillerie de la Ligne, Capitaine 1812
Boisselier entitled this plate to be that of a captain, but gives the figure the epaulettes of a field officer and a band of silver embroidery to his shako. The silver shako plate bears crossed cannon barrels and most probably these would have been surmounted by a crown.
Plate 249827. Source: Museum of San Martino.

TECHNICAL TROOPS

Train d'Artillerie de la Ligne, Conducteur, Grande Tenue 1812
Just why Bosselier has labelled the driver in this plate as being in 'grande tenue', is difficult to see. He wears neither plume nor shako cords. The shako plate confirms that the crossed cannon barrels were surmounted by a crown.
Plate 249872. Source: Museum of San Martino.

8

Internal Security Forces

From 1806 to 1814 there were thirteen Provincial Legions, plus the City of Naples Guard (which Boisselier captions in the plates by its French titles, Garde de Sécurité de Naples). Uniforms for the Provincial Legions, 1806-1814, were as follows:

Province	Coat	Facings	Buttons	Waistcoat
Basilicata	black	red	white	red
Calabria Ultra 1	black	red	white	red
Calabria Ultra 2	black	red	white	red
Calabria Citra	black	red	white	red
Lecce	brown	yellow	white	yellow
Bari	brown	yellow	white	yellow
Lucera	brown	yellow	white	yellow
Chieti	brown	sky blue	yellow	sky blue
L'Aquila	brown	sky blue	yellow	sky blue
Teramo	brown	sky blue	yellow	sky blue
Principato Ultra	blue	white	yellow	white
Principato Citra	blue	white	yellow	white
Terra di Lavoro	blue	white	yellow	white

By 1815 the provinces had been reorganized and all the legions were now to be clothed in dark green jackets and trousers. The military divisional numbers, into which the new provinces were to be organized, and the details of their uniforms may be seen in the table below. There were now 63 companies in the Provincial Legions.

Province	Division	Collar	Lapels	Cuffs	Cuff Flaps	Buttons
Terra di Lavoro	1st	orange	orange	orange	orange	yellow
Contade di Molise	1st	green	orange	orange	orange	yellow
Basilicata	2nd	green	yellow	green	yellow	yellow
Principato Ultra	2nd	green	yellow	yellow	yellow	yellow
Principato Citra	2nd	yellow	yellow	yellow	yellow	yellow
Abruzzo Citra	3rd	mid-blue	mid-blue	mid-blue	mid-blue	yellow
1st Abruzzo Ultra	3rd	green	mid-blue	mid-blue	mid-blue	yellow
2nd Abruzzo Ultra	3rd	green	mid-blue	green	mid-blue	yellow
Capitanata	4th	dull yellow	dull yellow	dull yellow	dull yellow	white
Bari	4th	green	dull yellow	dull yellow	dull yellow	white
Lecce	4th	green	dull yellow	green	dull yellow	white
Calabria Citra	5th	black	black	black	black	white
Calabria Ultra	5th	green	black	green	black	white

There were also Provincial Companies, formed of veteran soldiers, no longer capable of field service and employed guarding public buildings and maintaining public order. From 1813 to 1815 the Provincial Companies wore a uniform of dark brown, with facings shown on the collar, lapels, turnbacks and pointed cuffs as shown below. Buttons were brass and the turnbacks bore grenade badges in yellow or the coat colour. The shako had brass fittings and for parades a brown plume, with a tip in the facing colour was worn. White breeches and short black gaiters were worn and belts were white. The sabre strap was in the facing colour. Officers wore hussar-style boots. Facing colours for the provinces were as follows: Naples, yellow; Bari, scarlet; Capitanata, scarlet; Lecce, scarlet; Aquila, dark pink; Chieti, dark pink; Contado di Molise, dark pink; Teramo, dark pink; Basilicata, green; Calabria Citra, green; Calabria Ultra, green.

The Internal Security Guards were raised on 2 March 1813, but were not issued any uniforms until March 1815. The uniforms were the bicorn with national cockade, white edging and plume, dark blue tunic and breeches, amaranthe piping to the dark blue collar and cuffs, amaranthe turn-backs, white buttons and black gaiters.

MURAT'S ARMY

Gendarmerie Auxiliaire 1807
This is an unusually simple and sombre uniform and the man is heavily
armed, with a carbine, a brace of pistols, and a large knife.
Plate 249786. Source: *Bulletins des Lois de Royaume de Naples*.

INTERNAL SECURITY FORCES

Soldat de Police 8 January 1808
Another extremely simple, modest, practical uniform, with no frills.
Plate 249787. Source: *Ordonnances et Décrets*.

MURAT'S ARMY

Compagnie Franches des Chasseurs de Montaigne de Principato Ultra 1806-1807
The alternative title for this unit was 'Chasseurs Calabrais', and we see clearly that we are dealing with mountaineers in their daily costume, particularly the footwear.
Plate 249859. Source: *Bulletins des Lois de Royaume de Naples*.

INTERNAL SECURITY FORCES

Compagnie Departementale de Naples 1812
This soldier is depicted in grande tenue. The crossed bandoliers point to this man being in an elite company; the epaulettes in the facing colour are very unusual. The cipher on the shako plate should have been 'J' at this point and would have been surmounted by a crown.
Plate 249866. Source: Museum of San Martino.

MURAT'S ARMY

Compagnie Departementale de Naples, Officier 1812
The cap plate and the gorget both bear the crowned royal cipher, which should have been 'J'.
Plate 249869. Source: Museum of San Martino.

INTERNAL SECURITY FORCES

Garde de Sécurité de Naples, Capitaine de Grenadiers 1813
This is an amazingly elaborate uniform for a police officer. The central device of the plate on the bearskin seems to be couched on trophies of arms, that on the silver gorget is a gold grenade and the piping and plume are in amaranthe.
Plate 249867. Source: Museum of San Martino.

MURAT'S ARMY

Garde de Sécurité de Naples, Voltigeur 1813
The colourful finery of the various police forces of the city make the men of the army look positively drab by comparison. Plate 249864. Source: Museum of San Martino.

INTERNAL SECURITY FORCES

Garde de Sureté Intérieur de Naples, Hussard 11 March 1815
Despite this plate being labelled 'petite uniforme', this figure sports a cock's feather plume.
Plate 249860. Source: *Bulletins des Lois de Royaume de Naples*.

MURAT'S ARMY

Officier de Hussards de la Garde de Securité de Naples, Tenue de Societé 11 March 1815
This dress is also known as 'walking out dress' and he is wearing a 'surtout' tunic.
Plate 249862. Source: *Bulletins des Lois de Royaume de Naples*.

INTERNAL SECURITY FORCES

Hussards de la Garde de Securité de Naples, Grande Tenue 11 March 1815
The sky blue and amaranthe colour scheme is repeated here. At last, Boisselier produces a correct crowned royal cipher.
Plate 249863. Source: *Bulletins des Lois de Royaume de Naples*.

MURAT'S ARMY

Officier de la Garde de Sécurité Intérieure 18 March 1813
Apart from his plume, this officer would seem to be in undress uniform.
Unhelpfully, the gilt crest on the silver gorget is just a squiggle.
Plate 249861. Source: *Décrets et Lois*.

INTERNAL SECURITY FORCES

Hussards de la Garde de Sureté, Officier, Grande Tenue 1813
The finery of this officer's costume, from his cock's feather plume to the fox fur trim to his amaranthe pelisse, is almost overwhelming. He wears three silver chevrons over his cuff, indicating that he is a captain.
Plate 249865. Source: Museum of San Martino.

MURAT'S ARMY

1er Legion Provinciales de Naples, Voltigeur, Grande Uniforme 1814
Note the different greens of the uniform and its embellishments. There are no details shown on the tin shako plate.
Plate 249858. Source: *Bulletins des Lois de Royaume de Naples*.

INTERNAL SECURITY FORCES

Legion Provinciale de Capitanate, Grenadier, Grande Tenue 1814
The figure presents no problems, but the shako plate is – as usual – annoyingly blank.
Plate 249853. Source: Museum of San Martino.

MURAT'S ARMY

Legion Provinciale de Abruzzo, Officer de Voltigeurs 1814
The order of dress is not specified on the painting, but with plume and shako cords, it should have been grande tenue. No details are visible of the badges on shako plate or gorget.
Plate 249854. Source: Museum of San Martino.

INTERNAL SECURITY FORCES

Legion Provinciale de Basilicata, Grenadier, Grande Tenue 1814
Boisselier entitled his plate 'Batilicate', which is confusing. The figure presents no other problems, but – as usual – there are no details on the shako plate.
Plate 249855. Source: *Bulletins des Lois de Royaume de Naples.*

MURAT'S ARMY

Legion Provinciale de Lavoro, Officier, Petite Uniforme 1814
The original pre-1815 uniform colour of blue has now become dark green. The design on the shako plate seems to be a grenade, that on the gorget is yet another squiggle. Despite the title being 'petite tenue', this officer wears both plume and cords to his shako.
Plate 249856. Source: *Bulletins et Décrets du Royaume de Naples*.

INTERNAL SECURITY FORCES

2e Legion Provinciale de Calabrais, Voltiguer, Petite Uniforme 1814
The original pre-1815 black coat has now become dark green; despite the title of this plate being 'petite tenue', this man wears both plume and cords to his shako and these items were only worn for full dress. All the greens in his uniform seem to match.
Plate 249857. Source: Museum of San Martino.

MURAT'S ARMY

Compagnies Franches du Voltigeurs Abbruzzais 1807
This figure wears an extremely simple uniform, when compared to the 'buttons and bows' that adorned the Guard. He wears what the Austrians termed a 'Corsican hat', with an extended brim, upturned to one side, on which there may well have been a badge. His equipment is very much in the style of the *Jägers* of the German states of this period. He carries a carbine, much shorter than a musket, the barrel of which is probably not rifled.
Plate 249788. Source: *Bulletins et Décrets du Royaume de Naples*.

INTERNAL SECURITY FORCES

Bataillon de Chiarpa, Chasseurs Auxiliaires, 1806-1807
The dark green costume and black belts are definitely the hallmarks of this type of unit and he carries
a short musket, the barrel of which may have been rifled. His hat is a modified Corsican hat.
Plate 249789. Source: *Bulletins et Décrets du Royaume de Naples*.

MURAT'S ARMY

Chasseurs à Cheval Volontaires des Abbruzes, 1er Compagnie, Grande Tenue 1807
It would seem that no expense was spared when it came to attracting the local gentry to volunteer for internal security service; this elaborate, colourful uniform is most striking, if scarcely practical. This regiment also had plain red sabretaches, which is very unusual.
Plate 249790. Source: *Ordonnances et Décrets*.

INTERNAL SECURITY FORCES

Chasseurs à Cheval Volontaires des Abbruzes, 3e Compagnie, Petite Tenue
In the British army this form of dress would be termed 'stable dress', and would have been worn for mucking out and other fatigue duties. The white cap is most unusual, as these items were usually made up from old tunics and would thus have been in the matching blue.
Plate 249791. Source: *Ordonnances et Décrets*.

MURAT'S ARMY

Chasseurs à Cheval Volontaires des Calabres, Lieutenant, 2e Compagnie, Grande Tenue 1807
The two silver chevrons on the cuff and the white/silver top band to the shako indicate this figure's officer status. The plain red sabretache is most unusual.
Plate 249793. Source: *Ordonnances et Décrets*.

INTERNAL SECURITY FORCES

Gardes Provinciales, December 1806
This corps belonged to the para-military organization of the kingdom. Again we see the Corsican hat in use.
Plate 249792. Source: Bulletins of the King of Naples and of Marshal Massena.

MURAT'S ARMY

Eleve de l'Ecole Polytechnique 1807
This student of the Polytechnic School wears the black facings that one usually associates
with the corps of military engineers, for which he is presumably destined.
Plate 249794. Source: Museum of San Martino.

INTERNAL SECURITY FORCES

Officier, Ecole Polytechnique, 1812
The designs on this officer's shako plate and gorget are, unfortunately, totally unclear. The tasselled gold laces on the collar and the cuffs point to the elite status of the institution.
Plate 249810. Source: Museum of San Martino.

MURAT'S ARMY

Eleve de l'Ecole Polytechnique 1812
The uniform of this figure complies with all the details of the other two of members of the same institute.
Plate 249807. Source: Museum of San Martino.

INTERNAL SECURITY FORCES

Brigadier des Douanes Royales de la Ville de Naples 15 July 1807
The royal cipher 'JN' is correct for this corporal of the customs service, in his very plain uniform with a Corsican hat.
Plate 279795. Source: *Ordonnances et Décrets*.

9

The Navy

In 1798 the navy of the Kingdom of Two Sicilies contained 19 major warships of 30 guns or more, including six 74-gun ships of the line; 35 smaller warships; and 122 gunboats. The majority of these vessels were destroyed during the French occupation of 1798-99, and only a small number fell into the hands of the new rulers. The largest vessels initially available to Joseph and his successor were the 40-gun frigates *Cerere* and *Aretusa*, and the 30-gun corvette *Fama*. Along with smaller vessels, these ships were several times engaged with their Royal Navy counterparts in the waters off Naples during 1809 and 1810. On 18 September 1810, Murat, at the behest of Napoleon, planned to attempt a landing of 2,500 men at Messina as an *avant-garde* of a larger invasion force. The project failed miserably and Murat abandoned all future naval operations.

At Napoleon's behest, Murat revived the Neapolitan naval construction industry. New warships completed during the lifespan of the Kingdom of Naples comprised the 74-gun ships of the line *Capri* (launched 1810) and *Gioacchino* (launched 1812), frigates *Carolina* (launched 1811) and *Letizia* (launched 1812). An 80-gunner, *Vesuvio*, was still on the stocks at the time of Murat's fall.

The uniforms of the Neapolitan navy seem to have followed the lead of the French navy of the period, in that badges of rank were very similar to those used in the army, with the addition of the anchor motif in certain instances.

THE NAVY

Directeur Général de la Marine Militaire 15 June 1813
Just how the Director General of the Neapolitan Admiralty interfaced with the officers
of the navy is unclear, but this man is obviously not in a combat role.
Plate 249785. Source: *Ordonnances et Décrets*.

MURAT'S ARMY

Plate 249784 Compagnie de Gardiens de Marine, 31 January 1808
This term was used for trainee officers. The brass anchor badges on the collar risk being overlooked on the yellow cloth.
Plate 249784. Source: *Ordonnances et Décrets*.

THE NAVY

Eleve de 2e Classe de la Marine Napolitaine 18 March 1813
The rank of this naval student is shown by his trefoil shoulder strap.
Plate 249871. Source: *Bulletins des Lois de Royaume de Naples*.

MURAT'S ARMY

Artillerie de Marine, 1er Cannoniere, Grande Tenue 1 November 1810
The uniform is almost that of the field artillery, but the facings, plume, and distinctions are all amaranthe. The brass shako plate bore crossed gun barrels behind an anchor.
Plate 249782. Source: *Ordonnances et Décrets*.

THE NAVY

Artillerie de Marine, 2e Cannoniere, Grande Tenue 1 November 1810
This figure is identical to the forerunner other than the lack of fringes to the epaulets
Plate 249783. Source: *Ordonnances et Décrets*.

MURAT'S ARMY

Artillerie de Marine, 3e Cannoniere 1 November 1810
This figure is essentially identical to the two previous plates, but the details of the shako plate may clearly be seen.
Plate 249780. Source: *Ordonnances et Décrets*.